Anni Sennov

Love, Sex and Attraction
A Short Guide to a Successful Relationship

good adventures publishing

Love, Sex and Attraction
- A Short Guide to a Successful Relationship!

©2012, Anni Sennov and Good Adventures Publishing
First edition, first impression
Set with Cambria
Layout: Anni Sennov – www.good-adventures.dk
Cover Design: Michael Bernth – www.monovoce.dk
Author photo: Lisbeth Hjort – www.lisbethhjort.dk

Original title in Danish:
"Hvor svært kan det være?"
Translated into English by: David Tugwell

ISBN 978-87-92549-35-8

Contents

Introduction

Apart from travelling around the world or getting a good, personally challenging and extremely well-paid job, one of the major goals of many people's lives is to have a loving and well-functioning relationship, and this relationship must of course be with none other than *the perfect partner.*

Though few will admit it, most people go around with a secret dream deep inside them that one day *the big love* will show up and rescue them from their grey and dreary daily life. The big love is simply walking around somewhere out there, deeply lonely like themselves, and just waiting to meet that special person of their heart.

Suddenly one day there is a knock on the door and BANG, they have found each other and everything will be happiness and joy like in fairy tales and in the deep inner dream!

Well *love* does not always knock spontaneously on everyone's door, and maybe it is not the best solution for everyone suddenly from one day to the next to share 24 hours of the day with *the only one*, as there may be different factors and other people to take into account in your everyday life.

Many people today are too little aware of what they really want in their relationships and what the framework surrounding the relationship has to be like for it to be fully optimal for both parties and for any children they might have. They want to have love and all the good experiences, but they do not have a big desire to take on the many commitments that are often associated with a situation involving love and cohabitation.

Therefore to a much greater extent than before, more and more adult and mature people prefer to live a life where they are personally independent of their partner. They therefore consciously choose to live separately in this way so that each can better fulfill themselves in the relationship.

In this way they can more easily look themselves in the eye and defend the way they choose to prioritize in their everyday life, and as a bonus they also escape having to be accountable to their partner, who by virtue of their periodic absences do not have exactly the same claim on information about their daily movements, as would otherwise be the case if the parties lived together all the time.

This form of cohabitation is not strictly a male phenomenon, as you might have thought. It appeals just as much to many adult women with adolescent or adult children who have had enough of the paternalism they have previously experienced in relationships and now just want the space and opportunity to live their own lives without undue interference from their partner's side.

They have simply become allergic to constantly having to give account of their doings and goings, about their choice of friends and leisure interests, etc., and as payment for their personal independence they will gladly let go of the closeness and confidentiality to another person, which are two very important ingredients in a relationship.

So independence has its price!

<3 <3 <3

If you want to be *independent*, you have completely renounced the pleasures that a relationship can give in many areas, as an independent person is someone who acts *alone* and *in their own interests*.

In a relationship there are usually two to take decisions on behalf of you and the couple, and there are two to create the stability and continuity in your daily life together that is necessary for the joint framework to work in practice.

Independence in a relationship often leads to a lot of uncertainty between the parties as they do not always know where they stand. The only one who knows with reasonable certainty how an independent person will act is the person themselves. No-one else has any real influence.

But if you actually want *personal freedom* in your relationship – not independence – this can easily be reconciled with having a life together that is based on trust, confidentiality and intimacy, among other things. In that case you do not simply slip out of the door when it suits you without telling your partner where you are going, just in order to emphasize your independence. Instead you allow yourself the luxury *in good conscience* of informing your partner – and of course respecting any joint arrangements you might have and your partner's current needs – that you are just going for a couple of hours to be with some people that you have a great desire to spend some time with.

Freedom is a feeling that comes from within, and it is one which enables us to choose one thing over another without necessarily having an eye on other people's opinions and prejudices, or any possible unexpressed expectations they might have of us.

The urge for freedom only makes us uncaring if we *ourselves* want to be uncaring.

<3 <3 <3

Nowadays there are so many different ways to be together and cohabit, and living together as father, mother and child is not absolutely the most optimal form of being together for everyone. But despite the many different types of relationships that we are able to choose in our lives, there are actually very few people who dare to connect with their inner needs and live them out in the real world in full sight of everyone. But unless you do yourself a favor by finding out what you want at the deepest level in your relationship, you can easily end up doing exactly the same as so many others have done before you, that is, finding a partner who fits in well with your daily life and who you can have some lovely children with. On the side, you can find yourself a lover who suits you well sexually, and apparently none of these partners is *the big love* as then you would choose them 100%.

But why choose between a so-called *established relationship* and an *independent relationship*, if there is indeed something called that?? Why not just make sure that you choose *personal freedom* in the relationship right from the start, so that you yourself are setting the agenda for your life and your interaction with your partner and with other people in an honest and respectful manner?

<3 <3 <3

When have people ever been banned from thinking for themselves and articulating their own desires for life and their relationship?

There have always been people who have been the first movers in new ways of doing things, and if your way of coexisting has yet to be tested by others, who would be a more obvious choice to test it and live it out than you yourself?

May you have a free, happy and satisfying single or joint life which is matched to your innermost desires!

Anni Sennov

Balance in the Relationship

Responsibilities

The balance in a relationship is a balance in itself and it does not have anything to do with the personal balance of the two people involved. It can easily go wrong in the relationship even when one of the parties is doing very well. Some people are actually able to thrive in spite of the fact that they are involved in various imbalances in their job, family or relationship, because they can keep functioning well in other contexts.

But such an ability to abstract themselves from various vital issues makes this type of person a pretty unworthy partner in any situation – either at work or in a relationship – as they rarely support the other party when things go wrong. Their partner can easily come to feel lonely in the struggle to find a balance in the relationship, where the non-confrontational partner can often, without wanting to, end up in the role of the enemy in the middle of it all. And so the result is in a way already given!

Under more normal circumstances, people often break down in all areas of their lives in times of crisis in their job or in their love life. Most people find it hard to hold themselves up in one area when things are going badly in another, and vice versa, because it requires too many resources for them to pretend that everything is running normally when that is not actually the case.

But if the relationship is functioning in an unsatisfactory way whose fault is that? After all, it takes two people to have a relationship – or to run it into the ground – which is why there must also be *two* people to change things in a positive direction, if that is what you want. So both sides in the relationship have a responsibility to keep their life together working as optimally as possible!

Recreation

When you enter a relationship you should always remember that your partner has had a life before you even came into the picture, just as you had one yourself. You cannot expect that your partner will just drop everything they had been doing just because you have entered the arena. Not even if you might end up really missing each other many times during the day.

The world is calling, and maybe there are children, work, family, interests, and an ex-partner to take into account, so that in many respects everyday life can resemble a large and oversized jigsaw puzzle with many different possible combinations, where all pieces are guaranteed a place but where these locations must first be found and the pieces laid before peace can ensue for all the parties involved as well in the new relationship.

And maybe it is not the first time that the pieces have been moved around, so there may be some discontent among some of the parties involved, especially the children, which of course you also have to take into account when you make your moves in the area of the heart.

Mum or dad, for example, cannot regularly inform their children that there is now going to be a new boyfriend or girlfriend moving in tomorrow, without it having fatal consequences. So although you may have fallen totally in love, it might be the case that very much against your will you have to put a huge damper on yourself and your love needs, as they might otherwise clash violently with the wishes and needs of your children or other people. So often you have to go forward gently in a period where you have a great urge to do the opposite. So there may be uncomfortable amounts of stress associated with starting up a new relationship, no matter how great the love is or whether you are intending to move in together or not.

<3 <3 <3

Nobody can expect to get 100% attention from their loved one 24 hours a day, since time must also be set aside for each partner to be able to sleep, eat, work and relax, etc., as well as fit in any hobbies they might have. So the couple may be forced to have a serious talk at the beginning of the relationship as to how they can use the options available to accommodate themselves, their own desires and needs, as well as each other, as best as possible in the relationship. They may also have to talk about how much they might have to change the conditions in one or the other's camp in order to give the relationship the best possible chances of survival.

However, it is strongly discouraged that both sides should want to be the only thing that has meaning in the other's life, since such godly status could easily come to backfire at a later stage in the relationship, where the twosomeness might seem stifling and restrictive for their own personal expression.

Just try for a fraction of a second to imagine how it would be if everything in your partner's life related only to you? You can actually get tired of being the center of attention all the time. Just ask the royals and other celebrities who are constantly in the public eye, and who see themselves exposed in the media every day.

It may sound tempting to get all that attention, but it often shuts off the possibility of getting input from the wider world that does not necessarily have anything to do with you.

Recreation is therefore a *must* in the relationship if the interest between the partners is to remain high in the long run. For if you experience the same thing every day and you get the same thing to eat, then you will quickly reach a saturation point with each other. And if you do not have spice in your life at least *now and again*, the relationship will quickly become flat.

People – and especially those who are involved in relationships – have a need for experiences and external input coming into their shared world. There is nothing worse than two people being bored together. It is actually many times worse than when one person is bored in their own company.

Imagine if your relationship was already doomed in advance to a speedy break-up due to boredom. So you should do everything possible to have some experiences together, but also have some individually, so that you have something to talk about when you are together without one always knowing what the other is referring to – and vice versa.

It is actually a really nice feeling sometimes to look forward to being with your partner again after you have been apart for a while if only for a few hours, because then hopefully you will have something new and interesting to talk about.

Of course both of you should make sure you reserve good and ample time for each other, for a relationship should be continuously nurtured and nourished in the proper way. But for one reason or another it is not always easy for some people to do this, and then cohabitation is often turned into a struggle to get attention from the partner, whether it is positive or negative attention, which unfortunately is a *very common* story.

Respect

The biggest insult to one's partner in a relationship is to take their presence completely for granted. Similarly, you should not think that you know in advance what your partner intends to say in a given situation. It is one thing to love one another, but if love is not to be put to the test too many times, the best option is to ask your partner their opinion before doing anything on behalf of them or the two of you. For what if they have actually changed their mind since last time? Hardly any couples will get to talk seriously together every day, and it can be difficult to cover all points of view in fifteen minutes or an hour, or however long you have the chance to speak to each other, if both of you are to have an equal chance to comment. So one of you might easily change their opinion in a particular case without the other being automatically aware of it.

Some people also become more unpredictable with age, as they have nothing to lose on their personal account, in much the same way as young people often change their minds simply to provoke those around them. Of course, you have to relate to people like this as best you can, but in any case you should give your partner a chance to speak about themselves and their own attitudes before you make your point, since you are dealing with an adult who is able to think for themselves.

<3 <3 <3

In a relationship, make sure that you look at things as a whole and do not only listen to the things your partner says with his or her mouth. It is just as important to look at the actions and body language that accompanies the spoken word, as the signals here can be quite contradictory.

Everyone knows the situation where someone says 'yes' with their mouth, but their whole posture smacks of thinking 'no'. Of course you cannot be expected to be a mind reader in order to take part in a relationship, but often it would be a great advantage if you had such an ability to hand – and it would be even better if *both parties* had it at the same time!

Many couples have even chosen to base their relationships on non-verbal communication, where they do not need to verbalize their opinions for each other, as at any time each of them can understand the importance of a nod or a particular roll of the eyes from the other. Such well-developed body language is especially prevalent between couples who have lived together for a great number of years.

If you really want to have an influence on your own life and daily existence, you actually have a *duty* to express yourself – in your relationship too – otherwise you cannot expect to be consulted. This should be an ordinary daily practice between the two of you to show your respect for each other. For just as surely as you cannot speak on your partner's behalf without first having asked them, then you really cannot expect that they will automatically know what you are thinking yourself, without you having expressed it.

So in reality everyday communication is a way for the two people in a relationship to be able to express their deep respect for each other *if* the communication is actually allowed to go both ways in the form of a conversation!

Resource Allocation

In order to have a better overview of your life and to get a rough idea of whether you are getting the best possible benefit for yourself and others in everyday life, it is important wherever possible to divide your life up into units.

You should therefore think about yourself and your own personal needs, as well as the person you live with and the relationship as different entities, each of which should be allocated allotted plenty of time – and it should be quality time!

The family as a single unit with you, your partner, children, dog and parrot, etc. should of course also be allotted constructive time and the same goes for cleaning, gardening, the car, work, stamps, and your weekly swim etc.

With such prioritizing, the relationship, the family and your daily tasks do not have to end up being one and the same mass that you cannot keep separate in your thoughts because it all flows together due to the coincidence of interests on a number of fronts.

You cannot practice love for your children or the dachshund, for example, in the same way that you do with your partner. The latter can hopefully – unlike the others – stimulate the juices in the nether regions, so of course time must also be set aside for sexual contact.

The kids will enjoy having time with you – either the whole crowd of children at the same time or each child by themselves – without your better half necessarily being present. This is something that otherwise only happens in divorced families, but all families should provide space for it, no matter how closely knit they are as a family in their daily life. Mum and dad always behave differently when they are alone than when they are with each other, as all children know. And what child would not like to be given a higher priority than either mum or dad just once in a while?

And so children both as a group and individually should each represent their individuality independently of the family, in exactly the same way as your partner will.

As a single parent you should not try to play both father and mother at once in the hope that you will be able to replace the missing partner, as this often fails. Basically we have to accept that there are significant differences between the sexes and that men and women are therefore *not* able to contribute exactly the same kind of input to either the children or the relationship.

Of course, you can wear out your brain thinking about all the things that you *should* and *must* do in your life to keep all the different parties – including yourself – happy, and if you do sometimes get a bit mixed up in the prioritizing, it might be healthy to indulge yourself with a break for fifteen minutes without your partner or children for a change and get a recharge.

So it is important to set time aside in your life for your personal friendships and various acquaintances too!

You can have some fun and relaxation with friends and acquaintances, and with real friends you can share *everything* without getting into a fight about the dishwashing or laundry basket, etc.

In most relationships, friends can be characterized as 'yours', 'mine' and 'ours', though after the first few years an awful lot of couples restrict it to being only *our* friends. But it is just as important here as in many other areas of your life together to give each other space and opportunity to share your life and daily activities with people other than your partner.

Of course you do not have to have sex with everyone in order to have fun and to relax, which is why good friends clearly have their merits. And of course it may sting a little in your heart, and perhaps jealousy begins to stir in certain individuals when their partner willingly shares their most interesting life experiences with their best friends, without you even being involved in the stories. On the other hand, there cannot be many people who want to share *all their life experiences* with their loved one, no matter how much they love them, as you should be allowed to have *just a little private life*, even in your own relationship!

Giving each other freedom is therefore a matter of having some control over yourself, your self-esteem and your own needs, rather than simply measuring 'your value' based on the amount of attention that your partner gives you.

The Division of Roles

If the relationship is to have optimal conditions for survival, it is generally best if the parties have the same outlook, but also represent the other's opposite. In this way they complement each other in their daily life, instead of maybe fighting each other. For we must nevertheless remember that magnetism and sexual attraction are always greatest between two opposite poles. It is a relationship we are talking about, not a friendship, where you often understand each other particularly well and where the parties are always looking for support, advice and guidance from each other if the partner at home becomes too much.

A woman can talk to her friends in an endless stream – and for hours on end – and she can give vent to her many small daily frustrations and will very often receive great understanding and support for her opinions.

A man will quickly get tired of hearing these kinds of small complaints and chatter – perhaps because it is he himself who is often the topic of the conversation.

Should he still agree to listen to his wife's many small problems every day, it is far from certain that the attraction between them will continue. Many men choose only to listen to their wife with half an ear, which will cause most women to become completely blocked in the relationship. For countless women around the world, the consequence is therefore that they only choose to confide in their women friends – and not in their husband!

<3 <3 <3

Who plays which roles in your life and what do the various roles comprise of?

This is something that all responsible adults should be able to define for themselves if they want to get the most out of their relationships with other people and out of life as a whole. For if you are reasonably well aware of these relations, you avoid many disappointments on the road of life when people do not meet your expectations of them. For not the same is required from a husband as from a friend – or vice versa for that matter – and will it not be too much then for the woman to ask that her husband should play the roles of *real man with everything* and friend at the same time?

These are two roles that in many situations are likely to collide with each other.

Most women also have difficulties in letting the male hormone make its full entry into their lives so that they can pretend to be pals with their husband. For some reason for many people it is not natural to accept the role of the opposite sex if they do not have the physical and hormonal equipment in place for it.

But of course the partners should be able to talk together in their relationship. Anything else would be a disaster – and your women friends cannot be used as a rescue barge every time something goes wrong, so that a man totally loses touch with his wife's mental state, and she loses touch with how he feels about things himself!

The Domestic Balance

Expectations

If you only have yourselves to think about at home – you and your partner – then you might not think that this section on domestic balance has much to offer. But you should not make hasty conclusions, as most civilized people have a domestic balance to take into account, even if they do not have children and maybe do not even live with a steady partner all the time.

Most people have a desire to get their home situation, various obligations and their relationship to form a higher unity, and the balance between the couple and the home will thus come to have a large interaction on each other, no matter how much focus you have in your everyday life on jobs and eduction, or on children, money, sex and love.

Sex life
– with a special focus on families with children

Has your home sex life more or less stalled since the birth of your last child, and does it feel hard to spark up the relationship again, or as a mother or father do you find it difficult to relax completely with your partner in your most intimate moments together with the idea that your beloved child may suddenly be standing wide-awake in the middle of the doorway, and so share in *the adults' intimate life* at close quarters?

So, what is the problem? Must the child not see that mom and dad are happy with each other, or are you simply afraid to remove in one second the child's illusion that it is the stork that brings babies? In fact kids just have to see a few commercials and music videos on TV and they will instantly be better informed than this – and at a very early age as well! And what they do not know when they go to the nursery or kindergarten, they will soon learn when they start in school or the after-school club.

So why not just deal with things in the same way that they are done in many primitive societies all over the world, where you only have one room in the house and so *everything* is done in this room? And why not let the child sleep peacefully, although the child's bed is close to the double bed when the going gets hot between mom and dad?

In reality, this is a problem that belongs to the luxury department, as the one who is disturbed is not the child, but the adults – and that is you – and maybe your love partner.

If the problem feels *overwhelming*, however, then just accept this and move instead into the living room, out into the hallway or the bathroom – and even the kitchen can be used!

There are many excuses that can be used to avoid having sex with your partner, but the one about the kids does not hold water! Nor is it okay to let the various practical problems in your daily life affect your sex life.

Physical fatigue is what it is, but you should abstract away from your everyday problems and focus instead on your own bodily needs. Many problems can be solved a lot more easily after a good session of sex, because your entire system relaxes and various blockages are released when you let yourself go.

Physical illness and exhaustion, as well as mental disorders in one or both partners, along with the woman's heavy menstruation, are all of course acceptable excuses for avoiding sex. But apart from these you have to be really imaginative to find an excuse that holds water. The best excuses ever to avoid having sex with your partner are of course that you either do not love them or no longer feel attracted to them, or else they are violent, in which case you should keep your distance unless you are turned on by that kind of thing yourself. But if things have got so far, then the relationship must already be coming to an end in any case.

Unfortunately most parents with small children often need to get their view of the mother and father role turned upside down, as well as learning what it means to be part of a family while having a lover relationship with their stable partner. But many women and men are subconsciously afraid to address the concepts of sex and attractiveness in relation to each other, for what if your partner now livened themselves up to such an extent that they became interesting and exciting to people other than yourself. Or if they suddenly had to deliver something more on the sexual front because the partner began to make demands. Well so what!

Parents with young children often do not give themselves enough time for each other, and sex often feels like a pressure in everyday life because they constantly have the children around them, as well as a lot of practical work that they have to get done. It may therefore be a good idea for a period to have an agreement that attention to your partner need not only be given in terms of sex, but of course sex between partners should not be ruled out if it came to that point. The pressure of having to be physically available to each other is thereby considerably lessened for the partner or partners concerned.

It can also be a very inspiring solution to get a babysitter and take a trip to the movies, a music club, or go and eat out together. In this way mum and dad get some time for one another and a positive experience that brings them together, which often leads to a greater desire for each other. And the children get their *own unique* experiences with other adults or children away from their regular daily environment and routines at home with mum and dad.

This should not be exaggerated so that grandma is installed as a permanent fixture in the home for a fortnight at a time, because mum and dad should go on holiday together *again* and *without the children*. Just a few days is easily enough to boost the appetite between the partners.

Most adults have hopefully chosen to have their children and so it should also be they who take care of them as much as possible. So it cannot be a good thing to choose to be often without them – especially during the holidays, which should be the best time that children have with their parents either together or separately.

Setting Goals

Money, sex and love – how many people are there who do not have an imbalance with at least one of these three elements in their life, or have a daily deficit in more than one of these areas?

This will include many more people than meets the eye, and perhaps you also belong to this large group of people who have long since given up trying to change their poor situation in the area of money, sex and love, and so have accepted that life does not have much more to offer them in these areas?

If so – what do you want to do with your life in general? Because without money you will have no food on the table or roof over your head, without sex you get no children and no release for the body, and without love you have no content in your life – and so what is left?

You simply have to allow yourself to make some requirements of your existence and not stand idly by in the hope that others will do the thinking and legwork for you, creating the goals and ideals and maybe even making the pathway for you. Therefore you are compelled to activate your own brain cells and get your hands out of your pockets and tackle your life, for if you leave this important work and great responsibility to others, it will also be them who can take credit for the outcome and not you.

And the satisfaction is not nearly so great when things are the result of other people's work and a product of your parents' or your partner's personal ambition, compared to if you have yourself paved the way towards your goal.

The problem of setting goals in your relationship and your family and joint life is that you cannot always imagine what the actual situation should be in order for things to work properly. So you might be obliged to advance along the road yourself and try out the many different ideas and ideals in everyday life with your current partner and your children, before you can relate properly to how you want the framework to be, and how you prefer things to run.

And maybe you do not have to live in exactly the same way as most other people do, because at heart every family and every relationship has its own style!

<3 <3 <3

Some people live with one partner in their daily life and with another one in their hearts because they think that in this way they will have an easier time in creating a wholeness in their lives. At least that is often how it feels, until one day the balloon pops.

A situation like this is often due to the *partner in the heart*, who they love deeply, being either unable or unwilling to live their life the same way as them, so they instead choose to go out and find another partner to share their everyday life with. But the partner in the heart retains their permanent deeply-rooted place in their heart and will certainly be well remembered and loved forever.

There can be many reasons that separate the original loving partners in their outlook on life. Perhaps one party cannot live without security in their life, without other people around them, without constant admiration from their partner and their children and the need for the person's presence, without a lot of money in the bank, without sex and without a constant daily partner – whereas for the other party it is maybe just the opposite. And if you disagree about how those conditions should be integrated into your joint life, it is probably best to opt out in good time before you move in together, otherwise you will have invited various problems and daily power struggles into your life.

These circumstances very often contribute to the fact that many people offer more in their relationship than they had originally planned. They often transgress over each other's boundaries in such an extreme way – and without thinking about it – because they subconsciously know that the other party either cannot live alone or without the aforementioned situation being present in their life, and therefore cannot live without them as their partner. So if you have grabbed hold of your partner because of your thorough knowledge of their weaknesses, it is not love which is supporting the relationship, but the combative spirit needed to keep the other partner at bay.

<3 <3 <3

There are also situations where the two sides have no boundaries in relation to each other because they only feel responsibility for themselves and certainly not to the other. However, such relationships, if one can call them that, are quite exhausting for both parties since they never know where they stand.

If you want to cherish your relationship, you should always have just as much responsibility to your partner and your family as you have in relation to yourself – and here it is not just about what you can afford to offer the people around you in various situations, but it is just as much about contributing with new input, experiences, love, practical support and finances to the whole and to the community.

And of course your partner must then also contribute a similar effort in relation to the whole, so that the overall balance is maintained both in the relationship and in the home!

As for chores in the home, it is usually the case that the more we relieve each other with caring for the children and various tasks, the more time the couple have for themselves, for each other and for the family. So there will be much more extra energy to put into comfort, relaxation, sex and your interests – especially for the one who is bearing the greatest load – if the other partner puts in a bit more and gives an extra treat to their partner. For many people also have their regular job to do outside the home, after which they go home and continue to work there. So if you prioritize the concept of family time, time for the relationship as well as time for the kids, friends, hobbies, weekly exercise, and time to get your duties off your hands in a good and appropriate way, then the domestic balance will have the very best conditions to function in an optimal way, which you have read about in the chapter *'Resource Allocation'* earlier in the book.

Your Relationship and the World

A relationship has the best conditions to last first and foremost if the parties are attracted to each other sexually and have diffi-culty keeping physically apart and they also love each other; rather than if they first and foremost love each other and in addition are each other's best friends.

Relationships which are governed by attraction and love do not always seem nearly as stable and harmonious from the outside as friendship-based relationships. But it is this sexual glow that helps to keep the pot boiling and in the long term will make life together more interesting for both parties to stick to for a very long time and maybe even for their whole lives.

However, it is a matter of taste what kind of relationship you prefer.

Most people will probably connect the friendship-based relationship with slightly older people who have lived together for many years, but oddly enough many young people set out by putting the highest price and focus on stability and safety. This applies in particular to those around their 30s, when they suddenly find themselves being strangled in their self-made established framework with a villa and holiday home, two cars in the carport, family dog and rabbits in the backyard, two stable incomes and of course a couple of lovely kids.

It is then that they may no longer be able to put up with the status quo, the stagnation and feeling of being trapped, and so they are dying to *get out of their prison* at whatever cost. Now the time has come to go out and find the really big and sometimes uncontrollable love that goes directly to the heart and loins at the same time, and which can contain love, sex appeal and attraction in one and the same person!

Looking at the people who have courage enough to choose the partner who both their *heart* and their *loins* are stirring strongest for from the very beginning, we see that they do not always live to the standards that apply to ordinary relationships, and their relationship does not always look perfect from the outside.

These people accept it as a perfectly natural thing that life goes up and down, and they are by no means afraid to have a forceful and loud discussion, which might also be shared with the neighbors and children living at home, because for them *as a couple* it is more important to preserve the relationship, rather than consider what the people around them are thinking. And they know with great certainty that the relationship is not automatically doomed to fall apart just because they sometimes cannot stand each other for a couple of days. For they have experienced this so often that it has become a natural part of the relationship to make space for the two of them to feel a bit of hate for each other sometimes.

The fluctuations in the relationship are enough to give them a sense of *living*, and it is the bad days that help them to enjoy the good days even more. And from the overall perspective there can be said to be a balance in things, since the fluctuations appear to be equal on both sides of the center line. The most important thing is that the parties can jointly rediscover the balance in relation to each other whenever there has been a problem or some knot in the connection!

In this type of relationship the parties can even think of opting out when it comes to family events and the like where otherwise they would faithfully show up, if they needed to be alone with each other, or maybe only one of them will go since it is solely in his or her interest to participate in these activities. The couple can easily figure out how to be apart in their daily life without breaking down inside. On the other hand they enjoy being together whenever it is possible.

If the couple have children, who often are in the frontline when things go badly, then they will naturally be influenced by the things they see, hear and experience, but very often the children learn in this way more about life than they would do in thirty years out in the big wide world.

Children will simply have it confirmed that it is possible to love one another without being in total agreement, and they learn to tackle even insurmountable problems by themselves, which the business community in particular will value very highly once they become adults and are undertaking responsible jobs.

But of course it is important that the two adult partners in a relationship can get things into a higher unity in their lives nine days out of ten, or otherwise the children are at risk of being confused and frustrated.

On the other hand if we look at the children of couples who put a brave face on things at home, and who are mostly staying together because of practical circumstances and not really because they love each other, then unfortunately the children very often learn right from childhood to do nothing and simply sweep all the dirt under the carpet in the hope that it never returns.

This ability to avoid all the various problems is a very unfortunate feature to accept if you want a relatively problem-free life as an adult or a relationship based on honesty and openness to one another. In fact you will be a very unworthy partner in virtually all contexts, as shown in the chapter 'Responsibility' earlier in the book. For if you do not tackle the various problems as they arise and make a serious effort to resolve them, you will never get rid of them and so your personal freedom will continue to be hamstrung.

<3 <3 <3

The balance within the relationship is something that couples must themselves create as a joint enterprise, since they are the ones who know how they prefer things to run. But there also always exists an *even* more overall balance between the relationship and the wide world outside, which the couple should also take into account. And of course you must take into account the outside world, although it sometimes has consequences for your own little world at home, but then you do not have to attend all the events you are invited to, such as Christmas parties, parents meetings, girlfriend get-togethers, family birthdays and annual general meetings, etc. You simply need to prioritize in each case and sometimes say no thank you, if that gets things working better at home. But you cannot simply afford to cry off from any contact with other people because that fits best with your own stuff. If that is the case you cannot expect that the people around you will support you when you need it yourself, if it does not suit them to do so at the time.

There must of course be equal conditions for everyone if justice is to be done!

Problems in the Relationship

Problem Solving

A relationship is seldom a perpetual bed of roses, as many men and women are non-confrontational in terms of addressing conflicts and problem solving, especially when it comes to private matters. They often believe and hope that if they just leave their problems alone they will solve themselves, or else someone will come and solve them for them, just as their parents did when they were children. This is behavior that can drive their partner completely crazy.

Imagine the situation where everything is going completely up in flames at home and then your partner suddenly gets 'the brilliant idea' to go and have a rest or take a shower in the middle of it all as if nothing was happening.

In a situation like this it would probably be smart of you to ask the person who is disappearing how much they would like to be paid per hour to either help sort things out or else to sit down and talk the issues through with you.

Strangely enough, the person would not disappear in the same way if they had major problems at work, as then they would be guaranteed to be facing the sack at any moment. So maybe you should consider adopting the same rules at home.

Try putting this innocent little comparison between home and work to your beloved, as then they will probably get their act together for a time and put a stop to their thoughtlessness. But do not use it every time there is trouble brewing as the effect will quickly fade.

Even a subtle and humorous way of correcting your partner can turn into a habit and they will eventually ignore everything you say, whatever the degree of amusement, and then it becomes really difficult for you to slip through their defenses with your messages.

<3 <3 <3

If you have problems in your relationship, you need to deal fairly soberly with the facts, information and situations you are facing from your partner as well as from others. It is no use hiding all the unpleasant things in your subconscious as if they never happened.

If you want your problems solved and also want to influence the outcome, you have to do something about it yourself, or alternatively you may want to seek professional help.

It might be compared with trying to ignore your child's penchant for pinching things or hitting and biting the other children in kindergarten, simply because you cannot bear the bad feelings in your heart. But if you do not put a permanent end to the problems now, how is it going to turn out for your child in later life, for problems tend to grow in size if not caught in time. And the same holds true for any cruelty or unfaithfulness in your relationship.

Do not ignore things when they happen the first time, just because what you see or experience does not fit in with your ideal of a perfect relationship. Maybe it will happen again if you do not put the brakes on in time.

You should always mark out your boundaries clearly both in relation to your partner and others – if not before, then certainly as soon as they *go* or *have gone* over the line in one way or another. And of course you should also respect their boundaries in relation to you.

If you think that other people's boundaries are deeply unfair and have a bad influence on you and your life, you must tell it to the people concerned so that you can have a fair discussion about the facts. If this does not change your partner's views on the matter, it is then up to you to decide whether you intend to continue your life together under the given conditions or not.

If the relationship is already off track, you must be careful not to just stand by and wait for too long. Sometimes you can wait *a really long time* before things connect in a higher unity, and the question is whether the result was really worth the wait.

So it is healthy to have a good think every now and again, without there having to be a serious reason for it, about whether you still have anything positive to contribute to each other and whether you are happy with the way things are going in the relationship. People must act quickly if things start to go badly as relationships are an area of life that many people have generally *little* patience with if things go into crisis.

Many people think that it is easier to go out and find a new partner rather than repair the existing relationship, and that is just what they do!

Infidelity

It is always up to each person to decide whether they are *able* and *willing* to accept infidelity in their relationship or not, and when the decision is finally taken this should be reported as clearly as is humanly possible to their partner so that they are in no doubt about the position. You then have to just hope that your partner has the exact same position on this vital issue as you do yourself.

If there is disagreement in your attitude to infidelity, both sides should probably think about whether they have chosen the right life partner.

You can have a lot of opinions about infidelity and how you think you would react yourself if despite various agreements to the contrary suddenly infidelity one day become a reality. In essence one's behavior is hard to predict in the actual situation as so many different factors may play a role. So avoid making violent threats of fire and brimstone in advance, if your partner is cheating on you, because what if now you just completely break down instead of immediately throwing the deceiver out of the door.

There are those relationships where it can be healthy for the most dissatisfied party to find out *once and for all* – possibly through infidelity – that in spite of various notions to the contrary they are still quite happy at home. It is of course unfortunate that it is such a tough way for both parties in the relationship to have this fact confirmed, but the story has the best chances of ending happily, if for example the blunder was solely caused by boredom and irritation over trivial matters. And it can be guaranteed that there will be no infidelity in the relationship for many years to come – perhaps never – because the experience does not seem to have given the unfaithful party what they had hoped for.

Some men just cannot be peaceful in themselves and feel satisfied until they have been over into next-door's garden to have their way with the neighbor's wife. It simply *must* be tried!
But in fact it happens just as often the other way around, that it is the women who do not have enough of their own men at home.
These men and women obviously need to find out for themselves that the neighbor's lawn is not necessarily greener than their own, and that their neighbor's partner is not better than their own before they can have peace of mind. It is actually just like children who can only manage to keep their hands off the candle when they *have* burned themselves.
There is often a high degree of curiosity and greed, and a huge

internal discontent that is the basis for a pattern of action like this, which unfortunately tends to have an impact on the respect and humanity that the person should have for the person they share their table and bed with every day.

In return, you should probably consider whether you have made the right partner choice, if either you or your partner keep on practicing infidelity. Something is certainly wrong in the relationship, unless you have reported quite openly to each other that you are not *able* and perhaps not *willing* to live a life without affairs on the side.

There are of course relationships that can accept infidelity, because the parties have agreed to accept this as part of *their* way of being together. But there are relatively few places where both parties are equally satisfied with this solution, as they will rarely both have a different relationship on the go at the same time, and so at times they will feel abandoned and ignored by their partner.

It requires a high degree of awareness among all people involved to live with agreed infidelity – and in actual fact from the lover's side as well for they are cut off in advance from establishing a long-term relationship where the two of them can live together all the time.

Morality and Ethics

Ethics and morality are two very large pillars in people's attitude to infidelity in particular.

Morality is a set of rules more or less defined by society concerning how one should live in the respective community and the moral code may well be very different from place to place and from country to country. Morality is therefore a concept that you can take with a small or large grain of salt if the existing standards do not suit you in a particular place, as it is possible to move to another place where your behavior can be better accepted and where it might not seem unusual compared to the other people living there.

Where there is morality, there are usually also double standards, since unfortunately these two concepts way too often go hand in hand in many communities around the world, without people thinking of it as much of a problem.

For too many people have grown up with a lifestyle where the main thing is preserving a respectable façade no matter what – even if what lies behind may be less healthy or even rotten to the core – and it speaks for itself that the actions of these people often lie somewhat beyond the boundaries of both human compassion and decency – and perhaps even outside the framework of the law – simply because of the imprint they have had in their childhood.

For what good is it for people to pretend to have a clean and sober way of thinking and to be strong advocates for their beliefs in the daytime, when our Lord and the police chief have to keep their eyes covered as soon as darkness falls!

When morality falls apart for countless people, unfortunately it often becomes so loose that in many places it looks like these people are either playing a double game or leading a double life which their family know nothing about. For what these people say and think is one thing – and it is quite another thing how they behave in reality.

There can be a *very* large discrepancy between a person's public pronouncements and their corresponding actions, and with this fact in mind it may be hard to believe that infidelity, for instance, might vanish from the Earth's surface in the foreseeable future.

Let's just hope that you already *have* chosen or *will* choose a partner who you can fully rely on – someone who maintains a very high level of ethical standards.

For human ethics are about offering people exactly the same relationship as you yourself wish to be offered by them, while at the same time respecting their personal boundaries – even though they may not lie exactly where your own boundaries lie. For example if you promised not to divulge certain information, you should keep to this, even though it is perhaps only an insignificant detail in your own eyes.

Respect for the other person as an individual is paramount. But it is also important to take account of the whole, so that an individual's boundaries and wishes do not collide head on with everyone else's common position on things.

So in a wider circle you might easily end up taking specific account of an individual person in a completely different way than you would do in a smaller circle, or vice versa. This can be compared to the relations within the whole family and in the relationship which the family is built around. Here the partner cannot always expect to receive exactly the same attention and support when there are children or other people present as they get when the couple are alone together.

Forgiveness

With regard to infidelity a lot of people use the worst possible excuses for themselves in order to justify their actions. It is simply inconceivable how some unfaithful men and women can go around deluding themselves into thinking that their partner at home might also be unfaithful to them – and at the same time to see how they can take this single idea as a starting point in taking their just revenge. But it is equally inconceivable that these same people continue to believe that their partner at home has at no point ever got wind of anything suspicious.

Of course there are people who are completely unable to feel anything at all – and perhaps the unfaithful party is married to just such a person – but usually infidelity cannot be concealed from the partner in the long run, unless you are extremely good at covering your traces.

But even this trait may turn out to be so pronounced in a person that it has a bad smell of its own and then what do you do?

How about just once in a while trying to put yourself in your partner's place and thinking about whether you yourself would accept the behavior that you are showing to them.

Maybe the man or woman at home still loves their unfaithful spouse so much that they do not want or do not have the energy to rebel. The mere thought of perhaps having to leave the house, home and children in favor of the partner's new love can block any action by the person who is being deceived.

But there may be many other reasons that the partner at home might *quite consciously* allow themselves to be deceived by their partner. With their knowledge of the husband's or wife's hidden life in their back pocket, it may be easier for the deceived person to get their own way in various areas of their life together without too much struggle. Due to their quiet acceptance of the infidelity the person has gained power over their partner, and there are many more couples around that function in this way than you might think.

<3 <3 <3

As for keeping on practicing infidelity and being unfaithful, a large part of the world's population seems to believe firmly in the concept of forgiveness as a mitigating factor. If you have just once repented your sins, then without pangs of conscience you can just go out and continue where you left off.

However if you have 'sinned' on the sexual front, and you deep down regret your behavior, then for God's sake do not follow your first instinct and go home and confide in your partner, if you hold them very dear, just in order to be forgiven. It may well be that you will come to have peace of mind yourself, but what does your partner get?

Something to think about for a very long time to come, and in this case for the rest of their life, which of course would be deeply unfair if you do not intend to repeat the blunder.

It is only in the Catholic Church that you use this method to ease your heart afterwards, but there it is the priest that has to hear it, not the husband or wife at home.

If you are big enough to fool around with unknown men or women, you are also big enough to carry around the truth and responsibility inside yourself – or else you must either go to a psychologist, a therapist, or your parish priest to get everything talked out of your system.

In any case spare your partner, unless they have smelled a rat and are deadly keen on confirming their fears – or if you have a joint agreement to share all your agonies with each other, for then you have indeed wished on yourself some far-reaching problems in your life.

Imagine if now your loved one at home – quite unconsciously of course – *were to* use your transgression as a recurring theme for the rest of your life, or rather the rest of the time you two have together. Just the thought of it is unbearable!

Divorce

When it happens, a divorce is often very painful in different ways for those involved and the consequences are rarely the most comfortable, but in fact there are probably very few people at the beginning of a relationship who imagine that some fine day it *might* all go wrong. It is actually only in crime movies and crime novels, and perhaps in cases where people have an awful lot of money, that there is a definite speculation that it *will* go wrong. So it may indeed be a good thing to protect yourself in time for the sake of both parties with regard to how and what will happen with housing and finance, for example, if things do go wrong. For few people can predict exactly how they will react with a divorce – even if basically the couple are good friends and maybe still love each other. A lot depends on the specific circumstances.

One thing is certain and that is that you can always look at the conduct of the parties in a divorce situation and see how much they originally loved each other, for otherwise it will unfortunately soon reach the point where they try their best to do each other down and the thirst for revenge takes over.

If however the couple loved each other from the heart from the very beginning, then they will usually always maintain respect for each other in the crisis or divorce, unless they encounter something extremely terrible so that their respect is torn up by the roots. But of course situations will arise in the break-up which may be disappointing to the respective parties, no matter how much they try to take each other into account along the way, and this is probably the way it will always be.

When two people go from having lived a life together with more or less shared values and attitudes to life and then suddenly have to live their own lives separately with their own desires and standards, then the parties can often not recognize each other in the same way they could initially. And so you cannot be 100% sure where your ex-partner stands from one day to another in the aftermath of the break-up, as their surroundings are start-ing to get through to them much more than before with totally new and different input, simply because by virtue of their new situation in terms of relationships they have chosen to open up to the world.

Two ex-partners can thus risk just one week after the break feeling completely alien to each other, actually like two friends who have not seen each other for many years and where without realizing it they have moved very far from each other because they has not followed each other in everyday life.

However, if there is not a new opening in the relationship to the outside world in the aftermath of the break-up *on both sides* they will have very poor chances of getting on with their lives in a positive way, and this will be a most unfortunate basis to build their new life on.

<3 <3 <3

If all people chose their partner with their heart, then they would also listen with their heart if one day there came to be a rupture in the relationship in such a way that their mutual respect would continue to be maintained. This would also be the case even if they had to bear a number of disappointments from each other's side during or towards the end of the ailing relationship. Then they will not end up by perhaps accusing their ex-partner of having ruined *the perfect relationship*, for how perfect can it really have been if it could break so easily?

It takes two to have a relationship, and so it also takes two to give it ongoing care, and if the unfortunate circumstances arise that one party does not want to do something for either the relationship or for the couple, then it cannot be as exciting for the other party to continue the relationship.

For who wants to waste their time and their life with a person who will not contribute anything either to the partner or to the joint account? Everyone knows that there will always be people who in their deep naivety believe that their mere presence in the relationship is sufficient to make things work, but what are these people really thinking?

That the other person should do it all? If this is the case, these people belong to the large group of egoists who apart from themselves only their mother can love throughout a long life.

One should certainly not rely on choosing such a person as a solid partner in a love relationship. It can take an incredible number of years to beat their bad habits out of their system, while your own life passes by without much happiness.

<3 <3 <3

Many people in a divorce, both women and men, try to use the courts to completely destroy their ex-partner, simply because they feel humiliated and deceived or because they feel total despair over the situation. And they fight tooth and nail to get the maximum amount of money out of the break-up, at the same time as they struggle *completely without mercy* over the children. But if you basically still love the other person deep in your heart or at least have just a little emotion to spare for them, then you would not be able to bring yourself to display such behavior, which is why respect indeed ends up gaining the upper hand in many situations, just as soon as the people involved get time to think for a moment.

Merciless divorces often occur where one of the couple suddenly and without warning lets out their inner demons and in doing so proves to be a real bastard – possibly ably supported by their new love partner who has gained more influence on their life and attitudes, and thus also on the course of the divorce than is desirable.

But of course the ex-partner might have been unpleasant and unpredictable all the time. Love might have made one of the couple so blind that they were not previously able to see their ex-partner as he or she really was. If due to pure gullibility and naivety one of the couple has just been viewing the partner as they wanted to see them, and these two images are not exactly equivalent, then they obviously need to take a stand against their ex-partner – especially if their ex is constantly trying to breach their personal boundaries.

There must indeed be meaning with the madness, so that all parties – both adults and children – have the opportunity to get on with their lives on some decent and proper terms – taking into account their original form of life together and their original living conditions. The finances and time with children should be allocated fairly without any kind of disadvantage on one side, and there must naturally be optimal consideration of the parties' respective earning capacity or lack thereof, and any separate property.

It is an absolute *must* that first and foremost the utmost consideration should be given to best interests of the children and to the adults' ability to manage their everyday life themselves and look after their own children. It is of no use if the parent who gets full custody spends most of their time working and the children will therefore always be cared for by their grandparents or others, if the other parent has a lot more time to take care of the children.

Love, Sex and Attraction

Definition

If there is sexual desire between two people so that they cannot stay away from each other's bodies, and especially not from each other's loins, then this is obviously a very different situation than when we talk about *pure love* in a relationship. The rules of sex and attraction are in fact quite different from those that apply to love, and in reality there is no correlation between these two phenomena at all. However, one may choose to combine the two dimensions in one and the same relationship, which most people actually do, but in reality sex and love do not absolutely have to belong together for a relationship to be perfect.

Indeed as time goes by and they have put more dissolved relationships behind them, more and more people choose to base their new relationship *exclusively* on the sexual attraction between the sexes. But of course there are also opportunities to base one's relationship on *pure love* – where there is not any great sexual attraction between the two sides. This type of relationship is often chosen by people who feel they have known each other forever and therefore have some kind of deeper relationship to each other, which means that they just *have to* belong together. But such a relationship very often ends up being quite platonic, without either side being able to live without each other's company for that reason, and infidelity cannot always be completely ruled out as a valve in order to relieve the sexual pressure for either one of the couple.

Finally, of course, there is the complete edition which most people strive for in their lives, when you combine all three things at once – love, sex and attraction. And if you are able to combine these three ingredients in your relationship with the same person, it creates the basis for an optimal situation for living together, as each of the items has something to contribute in its own way to the relationship as a whole, which by no means can be got by choosing either love or sex and attraction on its own, for instance.

<3 <3 <3

Love is a very deep inner feeling or condition which for some people takes a very long time to reach, in some cases several years, whereas other people are simply able to open up their hearts in a split second.

Attraction, on the other hand, is related to some external conditions of the parties involved, such as their appearance and their physical and sexual needs, and in actual fact attraction has its source in the more primitive instincts in man that stirs *the animal* in us, so that the craving for sex arises.

Sex and attraction are therefore two very closely related states.

It is not known for sure whether the concept of sex in ancient times was exclusively created so that mankind could multiply and continue the species. But it is certainly the case that only a very small number of people in modern society today only think about having sex for that purpose in their everyday life. They prefer to use this rather enjoyable activity to release the physical and mental pressure that builds up in their system over a shorter or longer period.

<3 <3 <3

If you once experience love for another human being, you will actually be able to love them for a lifetime, almost regardless of what you risk being offered by way of unpleasant circumstances from the person concerned. Love is in fact completely unconditional in form.

The much-loved person has simply been lucky enough to get through all of your defenses and directly into your heart at a time in your life when you did not think about the possibility of being let down by them at some later point. But love does not need to only be something that binds two people together. It can also be used to set each other free. So you can end up having to conclude that you cannot bear to live with the person you love in your daily life, so you would rather set them free for reasons of *pure love* rather than destroy the feeling you have in your heart.

However, it should be added that love is not automatically reciprocated between two people. Perhaps it is only one side that loves the other and not vice versa, which is of course deeply regrettable, but as was already said if you love another person very deeply, it can easily feel right to set someone free in their life without requiring anything at all in return.

This is of course what parents do with their children when they are one day ready to leave the nest. The adults let go with pure love, although they may deep down wish that the kids could stay living at home with them for the rest of their life.

Actually it is wrong to say that you love another human being because of some very specific characteristics, because if you love someone unconditionally, it is difficult to point out exactly what it is about the person that you love most and what you like to a lesser degree. However you can feel attracted to some very specific characteristics of the person.

So if you love another person this will happen regardless of whether they make use of these particular properties or not, and this is basically the reason why many people stay in their relationships even though they may not find the partner's personal radiance and behavior particularly attractive any more. For such people completely forget to distinguish between the concepts of love, which sets people free, and attraction, which keeps people attracted and sometimes imprisoned by one another. Love binds them together in their relationship, though it should set them free in relation to each other, and by making things clear to each other in this way, it makes things much easier for them to make a definitive choice about whether they should leave their partner or not, rather than them feeling tied together perhaps to the end of their lives in an ailing relationship without mutual attraction.

Sex in the relationship

In order to keep the sexual excitement and spark in a relation-ship between two lovers there should ideally be a degree of entertainment present in the relationship. And actually it *is* possible to help a waning attraction back on its feet, for example by raising oneself up a little in the relationship and by making yourself a bit more exciting for your partner.

To get yourself to fight for the continued existence of the more intimate part of the relationship, you should really love your partner with your whole heart, and not just with your lower parts, although it is here that sexual life is centered for a large number of people. For if sex is the only thing that is binding you together, it is perhaps easier to go out and find a new playmate rather than staying and fighting.

The alternative is that *everything* ends up being about sex, which does not automatically leave any space in the relationship to allow everyday life to function together with the loved one – or whatever the sex provider should now be called.

If what gets you going is just having sex with another person, then it is entirely your own needs that you are seeking to satisfy, whereas when love is involved it is more a question of giving to each other and making each other happy. But many people often confuse these two phenomena in the hope of being able to explain why their own sexual needs may not always have something to do with their partner. But what is basically wrong with sticking by your own needs, as long as you also have space to do something good for your partner?

Two people who love each other and also feel attracted to each other normally always hope to get their love, sex life and attraction to go up into a higher unity in the relationship so that the needs of both parties to give and receive is satisfied to the greatest possible extent, either simultaneously or at different times.

<3 <3 <3

There are many ways to approach your partner when you would like to have sex. Some of them are very loving and attendant, others are intolerably aggressive and physically overbearing, and then there are those which indicate to your partner that now is the time when you can play, when you expectantly pull the whole toy shop and sex equipment out of the bottom of the wardrobe.

Actually sex toys should be an addition to an otherwise good sex life where the focus is on enjoying each other and not the toys. But many people eventually reach the *very usual* situation that they cannot really get turned on by their partner without simultaneously watching a porn movie or having half a toy shop hidden in the bedroom or in the spanking room, which they can amuse themselves with. They are simply using the equipment and *not* their partner to get a kick so that their sex life gradually becomes more and more artificial. For many people sex has completely degenerated into being an equipment and exhibition phenomenon and not something human, in just the same way as the clothes that are paraded on the Paris catwalks at the big annual fashion shows. There it is more about how the things look to the public and the media, rather than what use they have.

How the couple feel about having sex with each other becomes strangely less and less important, and so it is clear that the sexual needs over time become more and more extreme and kinky in the same way as Paris fashion.

There must always be something new to beat last year's collection, and the question is then what limits you intend to go beyond next year and the year after. In the real world there must be a limit somewhere as to how many variations you can have sex in before you begin to repeat yourselves, whereas for clothes it is probably harder to find the limit!

<3 <3 <3

Now having sex does in no way have to be a time consuming act in everyday life, nor does it have to require the greatest artistry and the greatest personal involvement every time. For what if one person in the relationship just needs to release the pressure? So give yourself time to this inspiring activity in your daily life, even if you do not think you have the energy for it due to overwork and stress.

But it should not be something you feel involuntarily committed to do every night, even though sex is basically a nice way for the body and head to relax. In essence the act should only result in pure pleasure, unless you have chosen a partner who has some different and/or sadistic inclinations.

If you are feeling completely worn out then let your partner know that you are not interested in the whole big thing. Then you have certainly been fair to them, and if it ends up with thirty good minutes of intimate coziness then nobody can complain. If instead you have the unmistakable feeling of wanting to just jump on top of each other and play rabbit then remember that there is another day tomorrow when you can hopefully spend more time together. It would indeed be a little cowardly to your partner if you simply stopped in the middle of it all.

For sex should not be doled out so that when I have spent ten minutes on you, then you should also spend ten minutes on me. You might think like that if you are only using each other for sex, but if there is love involved, then this intimate togetherness should be an extension of loving one another, in which case it would feel wrong to be ready with the measuring cup and stopwatch.

For love *cannot* be measured out!

A lot of women miss having emotion and love in their sex lives, and what can be said about that is that if the emotional part is not in place in daily life so that the couple regularly take the time to kiss and hug each other, then it is totally naive to expect that there will suddenly be feelings expressed just because the couple are having sex together.

For feelings and love are something that you either *have* or do *not* have for each other, and this cannot simply be forced to be expressed on special occasions, such as when the couple make love. So maybe you must be forced to conclude that there is a general deficiency in your relationship, which you must look at in an honest way and find a constructive solution to, or else you must unfortunately have to live with things as they are.

<3 <3 <3

If either you or your partner are continually sexually dismissive of the other person in the relationship because of various extenuating circumstances, then the partner will usually have to believe that this basic human activity does not have their partner's huge interest. And what do you do as the very understanding person that you are if you do not want to be a burden to your better half at home?

This almost gives you an open invitation, albeit not one that is formulated verbally, to begin to roam around in the big wide world in a more or less intense hunt for a lustful person who would be endlessly happy to acknowledge your sexual urges – and who will not make you feel guilty about having a basic human need for sexual release.

Actually it should be required of both parties in a relationship that they help each other to have an outlet for their sexual drives – except perhaps in situations where the couple's desires are very far apart. And in such cases you should probably consider whether there are grounds for anything other than a friendly relationship between the two, as it requires great understanding from the side of the partner with *desires* to accept to only have sex every now and then.

Correspondingly, it requires just as much understanding from the partner with *no desires* to give their body to something that they do not enjoy, or to accept that their partner will be sexually satisfied outside the home. And anyway who can live with these conditions over a great many years without feeling that they are missing something? It would certainly require that you love the other extremely much!

As a solution to their problem of not being able to coordinate their sexual desire for each other, some couples choose to have sex with either a third person or with other couples or larger groups outside the home, so that they can *jointly* put their possibly very different sexual dreams into reality. But this requires an extremely high degree of respect between the couple, and at the same time it requires a large acceptance and understanding of your own and your partner's underlying motives!

<3 <3 <3

There are not many people who will admit that there are sexual problems in the relationship, because of course it is only the neighbors who fight about such banalities. It is certainly not people like them!

A lot of things are blamed on the presence of children in the bedroom, the daily shopping and cooking, and there is also another day tomorrow that we should think about.

It is possible to make a lot of excuses.

Many adults – especially women – give themselves time every evening to read a bedtime story to their children, but why do only a minority of women come to realize that they can wake up again and get more physical and human benefit if they *figuratively* read a bedtime story for their husband too, and thereby get themselves a good and relaxing goodnight kiss?

The scenario may of course also be turned the other way around so the man reads the bedtime story for the woman!

It is not news that *everything* in a relationship turns into a habit and thus becomes boring if you constantly repeat yourselves, but then you can make use of this method just once in a while – or allow yourself to move the bedtime coziness to somewhere else in the house if this will make the act feel more exciting!

For you should not be beaten down by monotony so easily and completely lose your sexual appetite just because boredom has made its inroads into the relationship – then it might be better to change the menu a little if that makes the food go down more easily. But it is clear that if you continue to find your partner more or less unappetizing then you should probably consider changing them. But it might help a little to think back to the good qualities of the person that you fell for all those years ago, in order to put some pep into your appetite for both love and the physical act. Alternatively, you should simply make an appointment with your partner that you live together as friends in daily life, but that sometimes you have to go down in the city alone *to get yourself a little space*. And then let's see how long you can live together with this model.

But why not just decide for yourself that you will make your sex life an area where you just want to succeed, even if it means especially as a woman that you must accept that your beloved husband or partner cannot always spend hours on you first so that you should get something out of it before he finally gets his turn. Sometimes he might have permission to get right down to it without showing any special and extraordinary care to you. Actually a bit like in 'The postman always rings twice', where the woman is completely taken with her panties down, but she enjoys it anyway. As a woman you should maybe only do this for a change, knowing that you obviously can only accept this behavior from your permanent partner if he loves you unconditionally day in and day out, and you also find something fascinating in the experience.

But you should not make yourself available in this brief way to any man in town on Friday night just because you are a woman, unless it is a definite urge that you feel inside yourself. For there is rarely any long term benefit associated with this type of behavior, unless you become pregnant afterwards, if that is what you really want.

With your permanent partner you know as a woman that there is a new day tomorrow where he can take care of you in a loving way. And if in some strange way he ends up going and forgetting your so-called intimate needs, you just have to open your mouth and communicate your noble desire to him in such a direct way that the message is first understood and then followed.

No man likes to hear that he is inadequate at home on the colored sheets.

The quick lay where the man just jumps on top, so to say, clearly has its charms, but seen with the woman's eyes, it should not be an integral part of the couple's intimate program, unless the woman herself is quite crazy about it. Otherwise she can very quickly begin to feel like a service provider – and there is considerable difference in a relationship between providing services and providing love!

Freedom in the relationship

Many people do not much like to run their relationship and home life according to a timetable for the sole purpose of getting things to go up into a higher unity in their daily life. In fact it is only when they have children that they can see the usefulness of such prioritization. The alternative is that everything around them begins to get messy, both physically and also with appointments and suchlike, and then the personal freedom in the relationship becomes compromised.

In such a situation you can very quickly come to feel like a prisoner in your own home and in your own family, where the bogeyman role is played solely by your partner, who has to be the one causing *all* the problems. It is certainly rare to even feel that you have played your part in things moving in a negative direction.

However, if you relate quite logically to the concept of *relationship*, it is clear to everyone that it needs an overall structure as well as some solid framework and agreements to prevent the partners themselves, or their children, wasting too much time waiting for each other in their daily life. Nevertheless most couples continue in pure ignorance to live life so that love in the relationship can *flow freely*, without the practical things taking over, and unfortunately what then happens is all too often just the opposite of this beautiful intension.

For many people refuse, often with their subconscious mind, to relate in exactly the same way to their relationship and love life as they do to their work and hobbies, for example, where you have to schedule your time for the sake of other people. But your partner and your family are *also* other people – it is just that they are not strangers – which is why you should of course take as great care of them as you do with all the other people in the world.

Your home is not just a place that you can afford to take for granted. In reality it is a little company in itself, which must of course be properly provided for both in terms of employees and finance, etc., while at the same time hopefully everyone involved is happy being employed in the company.

It may therefore *be necessary* to reach agreements on who is doing the shopping and washing the clothes, and who is driving the kids to dance and sport, etc., and talk about whether it is appropriate to take part in some engagement or other if you do not want to risk being too disappointed with each other. These are disappointments that have nothing to do with love, but rather relate to practical circumstances.

<3 <3 <3

It is very important in a relationship to be able to assign quality time that the couple can spend together without other people also being present. Of course it is nice to be able to relax with your children and with good friends and the rest of the family, but if you cannot figure out a reasonable way for just the two of you to be together then you have a problem in your relationship.

In the same way, you should also set aside constructive time for your children – and preferably where both father and mother take turns to do different things with them – so the children do not always have to share their mum and dad with the other parent or with whoever may be visiting the home. Even children can get tired of guests visiting all the time!

It is also equally important, however, that both parties set aside time to be exclusively by themselves, while the partner and/or the rest of the family takes a trip out of the house for a day or two, so that they can quietly potter around the house and have the whole place to themselves. And it is this privilege, or this freedom in the relationship if you will, that only a very small number of people allow themselves or each other.

Having freedom in your relationships does not mean that you can just choose to be without your partner and your family at your sole discretion when it fits in with your own stuff.

Having freedom in the relationship means having some influence on how your joint life and your everyday world runs, and therefore it also means that you yourself can help to develop the premises that everything is based on. And in this connection there is nothing wicked about announcing that you have a great need for time to be by yourself. Your partner could of course refuse this *when* and *if* they think the limit has been reached.

Freedom in the relationship does not automatically give one party the right to run around in town and have fun all the time, while doing their utmost to get out of doing chores at home. For if this person lived alone, their daily life would still have to be taken care of and their duties carried out, which has an influence on the degree of freedom in everyone's life. And the dishes would never get washed by themselves without help from human hands, for even a dishwasher needs human hands to be filled and emptied again.

The sticking point is therefore about the agreement you enter into with your partner in the relationship – both right from the very beginning, but also later in the relationship. In this context it is best to be as honest as possible with each other, so that at some later point you do not have to use time getting out of various falsehoods or concealments, which can do a lot of harm both to yourself and your partner.

If you are honest from the very beginning, you obviously run the risk that the relationship will either never materialize or that it quickly goes down the drain, but that is better than having to live a lie all your life in order to adapt to another person. For honesty makes a real basis for the couple to build their joint lives around, instead of each one all the time having to cope with new opinions and expressions from the other, which can upset the original balance in the relationship and create ongoing stress and insecurity among the couple.

<3 <3 <3

The feeling of freedom is an inner state which the people around you have no real influence on. If you are always honest to yourself and only choose to do what you feel is right yourself, then there is no danger that the feeling of freedom will disappear from your life.

Of course some times in your life you can feel pressured to make some choices which you either do not feel comfortable with, or which are not fully consistent with your inner convictions, but then you usually do everything you can to quickly get back on track so you can feel comfortable with yourself again.

So you can easily choose to attach yourself to another person – possibly via a relationship – even if you care a lot about your personal freedom. For the mere fact that you have chosen your partner yourself means that you can still feel free inside and be satisfied with yourself.

In reality all that happens is that there are two of you in your daily life instead of one; and when children arrive, it becomes three, four and five instead of two, it is as simple as that!

Feeling free in your relationship comes from being honest with yourself and true to your own opinions. And if you are comfortable with yourself and with your own choices, then you will not be afraid to take on different types and degrees of responsibility, since

PERSONAL FREEDOM MAKES RESPONSIBLE PEOPLE !!!

You actually first get personal freedom the moment that you are able to define your own boundaries for yourself, and also dare to report them to other people and stand by them in relation to yourself and to the world. And this is where responsibility comes into play.

For if you are responsible to yourself and to the things that you yourself are responsible for, it will feel *no problem* to be responsible with respect to other people both in your relationship, at work, and in relation to your children!

Personal Radiance and Energy

Are you MASCULINE or FEMININE
– and what is your partner?

Having broad shoulders, lots of hair on the chest and very large upper arm muscles is just external confirmation of a man's male sex – you can say he exudes a lot of *manliness* – but these pieces of equipment do not automatically make him a very *masculine* man.

And being equipped with good hips and some of the best breasts in town is also external confirmation of a woman's sex – she simply reeks of being a woman from a great distance – but these attributes do not automatically make her a *feminine* woman. In fact, she may well be extremely masculine in her energies.

This is because the concepts *masculine and feminine* are related to human *attitude and behavior* irrespective of their gender. In fact our masculine and feminine energies are connected with *our power of attraction* to those around us.

Body shape on the other hand is largely determined by gender and genetics, which often means that the tendency to belly fat and hanging breasts goes down through the generations without much chance of altering the physical result.

It is possible however to change your personal radiance and your attractiveness by working with your psyche and your consciousness, so that both men and women can end up having a better balance between their masculine and feminine side. It is also always good to know the extremes at either end, either through yourself or through others, as this makes it easier to tell when you have arrived at a balance. If you know yourself well and feel good about yourself, then you will naturally function much better in relation to the outside world and especially in your relationship than you would otherwise.

Many men do not care to have their personal radiance labeled with the term *feminine* – indeed they find it pretty derogatory – unless they have participated in a number of advanced management courses where they have been shown the various advantages of also having the feminine traits embedded in their personality. For their intuition and understanding of the world would be completely missing if they did *not* possess any feminine energies. As executives, they would also be doomed in advance in their highly responsible positions if they only possessed the outgoing *masculine* vigor and completely lacked the *feminine* overview. So it is clearly an advantage to have a balance between the energies.

The fact that a man appears *wimpy or effeminate* is seldom due to a predominance of feminine energy, though that is also a possibility. His *wimpiness* should rather be attributed to perhaps *not much* of a manly appearance, and the fact that he might dress in unisex clothes that could just as well be worn by women.

Curiously enough young women dressed in smart-fitting clothes are seldom called *tough*, although they may turn out to be some very tough rivets indeed. It is more common to refer to women on motorcycles and dressed in leather as being tough, even though they may be very mild by nature, but just enjoy having a combined cocktail of fresh air and high speed.

Whether people are wimpy or tough, masculine or feminine, seems often to be assessed on dress and appearance alone, rather than on the person's appearance and behavior. In fact it is just the same as when *a well-equipped man* with good arm muscles, etc., is referred to as *masculine* by the women swarming all over him, before they have even exchanged a word with the man and given his personality any closer examination. Imagine if he is actually a terrible fusspot and a huge egotist at home, who is simply very conscious of his great attraction to women when he is out on the town.

A man like this is *not masculine*. In fact, he is far from being *a real man*, and possesses a high degree of *feminine* conscious and very calculating energy, even though you may have first to visit him at home to spot this.

In fact it is no wonder that so many relationships go down the plughole once the couple have to function together in everyday life. For you can go very wrong at first glance and assign to a potential partner some very specific properties solely on the grounds of their looks and body type, and then things are bound to go wrong. For instance, a very gentle man with a very manly look does not want to constantly act pure macho just to satisfy his partner. He will very quickly tire of this kind of role-playing if it is far from his original nature.

To find a partner that fits you like a glove, it is definitely a real advantage to know your own energy structure before you enter into a relationship. This will avoid many unnecessary problems to do with understanding why your partner acts like they do in certain situations.

Are you *masculine* or *feminine*, or do you have a nice balance and a good interaction between these two energies? In order to make the relationship last there should preferably be an overall balance between you and your loved one where you complement each other in the relationship instead of fighting each other. Magnetism and sexual attraction are in fact always greatest between two opposite poles.

It is a couple relationship we are talking about, not a relationship with your best friend who you can tell your complaints to when your partner at home is too much.

On the following pages you will find an overview of how the masculine and feminine energies behave in their very pure and extreme forms in a variety of interesting situations. This will give you a basis to evaluate yourself and your loved one, so you can find out if you suit each other at all and whether you are able to complement each other in daily life.

The overview is not divided by gender, since the respective energies are expressed in much the same way in men and women:

Relationship

The MASCULINE man or woman

A great charmer who loves to seduce masses of men/ women with gifts and flowers and good food, etc.

The person has 'grand gestures' in the rutting period, but is not particularly stable with regard to psychological support in the relationship in the long run.

They simply hate crises and always strive to maintain a respectable façade.

They are cooperative if others come with tips that are easy to put into practice, and actions such as: "kiss me" or "make love with me" – but otherwise not.

The FEMININE man or woman

They are difficult to seduce without a fight, unless they themselves have singled out their victim.

They prefer community and depth with the 'real one' and often suffer from jealousy over the partner's past.

Deep down they want to have their partner all to themselves and do not throw around phrases like "I love you", as things like this can be seen in the person's eyes.

They love outstanding and unique experiences and are on an eternal hunt for them.

Sex

The MASCULINE man or woman

They are turned on by a partner with lots of charm and the right attitude in relation to the outside world, as well as to a shapely butt, sexy underwear, and the way the butt looks in the sexy underwear.

They are also turned on by their partner's looks and react with lightning-fast spark, ignition and subsequent release, and they are close to being a wholesale consumer of sexual paraphernalia.

The FEMININE man or woman

They have a lot of power over their sexual energy and they can actually manage themselves to reach an orgasm – or to completely stop.

They love power in the situation and power over their partner, and some fantasy porn movie is often running through their head, which in an interesting way can help to support the external act when they are having sex with a partner.

They are either bashful or very bold in their sexual expression.

Home and Interior

The MASCULINE man or woman

"My home is my palace" and therefore it will be on display to anyone who will bother to admire it.
The style of an interior design magazine is followed to the letter, and the 'right' artwork is hanging on the walls. It is always very tidy when a visit is expected, but do not dare to show up unannounced on an ordinary busy workday, as then things may be all over the place.

The FEMININE man or woman

"My home is my fortress", where only the chosen few have access.
The person puts their very own stamp on things, and so the home is characterized by a very personal style. There might be a lot of mess until things have found their final place, but then everything is straight and perfect, and there is nothing falling out of the closets.

Holiday

The MASCULINE man or woman

They like to hold their vacation in well-known locations which have been warmly recommended by other people. They must see all the tourist attractions that are there – if only to say afterwards that "I've been there too!" They prefer sun, summer and warmth and have a tendency to get holiday stress.

The FEMININE man or woman

For holidays they prefer to go their own novel ways. They love peace and quiet and often look for places that no one has visited before. However, they prefer their holidays in cooler spots where you can breathe easily and they would be happy to go totally alone.

Sport and Leisure

The MASCULINE man or woman

The person has an active leisure time with many activities and lots of socializing.

They prefer fast-paced and competitive team sports like football, handball and basketball, where they are part of a team and can move or hide in the crowd depending on the outcome.

They love socializing after the game – and especially with beers and entertainment.

The FEMININE man or woman

They prefer individual performance activities such as golf, chess or cycling, where precision, overview and stamina are most important.

These people are captivated by virtually all types of mental challenges when it comes to *figuring something out* and beating their own record, and they love speed if they have a car or similar to race in.

They can spend a long time philosophizing about life and they are more than happy to work in their spare time.

Friends and Parties

The MASCULINE man or woman

They are friends with everyone and love partying.
The more the booze is flowing, and the bigger the hang-overs will be, the better the party.
They are very social and like to follow the style that is suitable for the place where they are at a given time – even if it could have extremely adverse consequences the next day.
"If the others can, so can I!" is what they say, and so there is always a risk that things will go wrong, something that the person often comes to regret afterwards.
They do not realize the consequences of their actions until it is *too late*.

The FEMININE man or woman

They have few close friends that they share *everything* with.
They rarely hold a party, but when it happens there is preferably *a very special* reason for it.
The menus are carefully laid out, and the guests do not always have much in common with each other, but it will always be interesting!
If the boundaries are to be exceeded, then it always happens in a fully conscious and sober state.
"We'll have no drunken Christmas party with all the

infidelity here. I'd rather be intimate with one of my colleagues on a Wednesday, when I'm completely in control of myself! "

They are always conscious of the consequences of their actions *before* they are performed in real life.

At Work

The MASCULINE man or woman

They are often employed as a salesperson and serve as the company's public face.
They are able to keep up small talk for hours.
The person really wants to be popular with their boss, colleagues and customers and so often tells them what they want to hear.
They are clearly best at all the easy work, where there is a clear sense of getting things done.
They really appreciate after-work fun and all kinds of course activities, *when something happens*, and if they are the boss they love to act as pals with their employees and are keen on innovations and new projects.

The FEMININE man or woman

They are often employed as an accountant or in the company's backroom staff, where they have control of the finances and product quality and can keep an eye on the employees' daily work.
They are generally more concerned with their work than with their social life in the workplace, and they are able to immerse themselves so completely in a task that the people around them may feel completely cut off from the individual's universe.
They are happy to fight their way along the long and

narrow path to the top in order to gain authority, and they love competition where the battle is based on knowledge and insight, as well as stamina and mental awareness.

Appearance and Dress

The MASCULINE man or woman

They always adapt their attire to their surroundings.
They wear their work uniform to work and their party clothes to a party.
They simply love to be seen and if they are a woman they do not go out of the door without make-up.
They are very keen on looking 'proper', and therefore are often dressed in branded and classic clothes or magazine style, which they are more than happy to buy at a discount as long as the people around them don't know it.

The FEMININE man or woman

They often have their own unique personal style, which may however change from time to time depending on their mood.
The same can be said about make-up for women if they wear it.
Their clothing is only matched to their surroundings if this fits into the person's own style, for "you have to be your own person!"
In general they are happy to spend a lot of money on themselves, unless stinginess has become a fixed part of their lifestyle.

Practical Guidelines
for Love and Attraction!

Question

What can I do and how should I react if I meet a man/
woman who I then find impossible to get out of my mind?

Is it LOVE?

You can usually only talk about love for another person
when some time has passed, and you have seen them
from their worst side. If you still find the person lovely
then it must be described as love.

Is it ATTRACTION?

There has clearly been something in the other person
that you have been attracted by, and unless your loins
feel quite dead at the thought, it may be a case of sexual
attraction. It is then up to you whether you want to do
more about this.

Question

What can I do and how should I react if my loins cannot keep still when I think about or am in contact with a particular person?

Is it LOVE?

There is such a thing as love at first sight, but in this context it does not usually mean that the loins would necessarily get going.

Is it ATTRACTION?

It is a basic sexual attraction, where it is perhaps just a case of testing things out. Fortunately feelings of this kind often apply to both of the people involved at the same time. But if it is absolutely impossible to follow up the affair, then get as far away from the person as possible and in a hurry, and then think back on the experience as confirmation that your vital parts are still alive.

Question

What can I do and how should I react if my heart beats wildly and the butterflies in my stomach go crazy when I am with or thinking about a particular person?

Is it LOVE?

It sounds like you have fallen in love with them and are deeply in love. If you are able to do something about the situation, then go all in even though you risk it being over tomorrow, and you will feel hurt for a while. In any case, at some point you will come down to Earth again and get yourself under control, regardless of whether a steady relationship has come out of it or not.

Is it ATTRACTION?

It certainly sounds like a bit more than just attraction, and your greatest wish at the moment is certainly that you two can come to share *everything* with each other without having to take any notice of the outside world. But this is probably not going to happen, no matter how much you like each other. There is always a world out there that tends to put its oar in at the most disturbing moments, which in your case will be almost all the time. Enjoy your butterflies and know that at some point they will begin to fly in formation so that you will regain control of yourself.

Question

What can I do and how should I react if I want to get in contact with an attractive person, but I did not immediately perceive a positive response from them?

Is it LOVE?

You should always respect others' statements, whether these are for your personal benefit or not. You will have no joy from being with someone who does not find you attractive enough. So you should move your focus to other people and places instead.

Is it ATTRACTION?

Apparently the attraction is only happening on your side, so you should stop and do nothing more about it. There is no need to subject yourself to unnecessary disappointments and eventual rejection. Another bus will always come along with new opportunities, so just be patient and wait a bit longer – and if you cannot do this you will have to make a visit to the nearest nightclub instead and study the daily meat market.

Question

What can I do and how should I react if I have got the hots for my married neighbor?

Is it LOVE?

Try to keep your private parts to yourself for the sake of you and your neighbor's respective partners, unless you are absolutely determined that you simply must have this person at whatever cost – and let's hope that they also want you. If you both have children, you will of course have to look your respective ex-partners in the eye for many years to come. It is a bit like running away with your best friend's partner where things are simply too close and it therefore creates far too many painful dislocations at once.

Is it ATTRACTION?

If you really loved them very much, it would be a question that only you and your dear neighbor would know the answer to. Instead you will just have to daydream a little about them sometimes and leave it at that. And for God's sake don't just stand staring over the garden fence all the time.

Question

What can I do and how should I react if my partner has been unfaithful to me?

Is it LOVE?

Despite the fact that you feel deeply hurt, it can still pay to fight for the relationship, if you still love your partner that is. Try to find out why things went as they did. Is it because they like to sleep around a lot? Was it a squalid mistake? Or have the pair of you forgotten to show that you still love and feel attracted to each other? If it is the latter reason, look at the experience as an indication that you should be there for each other every day, and that both of you must focus on making your everyday and married life more exciting.

Is it ATTRACTION?

If this is behavior that your partner has practiced repeatedly, you should probably ask them whether they still love you at all. Love is equal to respect, and therefore your partner should be big enough to say at home if they have a problem with resisting being sexually attracted to other men/women. If your partner is not getting enough sex at home, despite their considerable need for it, infidelity is a natural reaction. Alternatively, you must work together to find a more

stable solution to keep both parties happy.

Practical Guidelines for Love and Attraction!

Question

What can I do and how should I react if I cannot keep myself under control in relation to other men/women?

Is it LOVE?

You should actually be ashamed of yourself because you should not practice infidelity in a love relationship without first having an agreement about this with your partner. If it is actually because you are sexually undernourished, then you have to say this at home so that you can look at the situation in a fair manner and jointly find a good solution. If your partner has a great deal of love for you but very little sexual need, then maybe it might be suitable to have a fixed agreement to go out on the town, but not without permission from your partner at home.

Is it ATTRACTION?

If the horniness or infidelity is solely to do with attraction, you are probably only doing it in order to be confirmed. If it is rather a question of not getting enough sex at home, you should probably consider whether you are either too demanding or if your partner is insufficient for you on the sexual front. If the latter is true, we can at least hope that there is still love present as otherwise the relationship is a total waste of time for both parties.

Question

What can I do and how should I react if I dream about being with a man/woman who is not my permanent partner?

Is it LOVE?

You appear to be mightily bored in your relationship, which is a pity, and as you know that your partner will be sad to hear about it you should keep your thoughts to yourself. However, it is truth that allows you to go furthest in a love relationship. If you love your partner, it would be healthy to convey your innermost desires to them – whatever they might be – so that you can jointly find a solution as to either how it can be satisfied or what it takes to make your relationship more exciting. Should you against all expectations make off with another partner, then for heaven's sake keep your mouth shut at home and spare your partner your guilty conscience – even if you have to bite your tongue and take the knowledge with you to the grave.

Is it ATTRACTION?

Then there is nothing else to do but to jump into the deep water and try things out. But think about it, because what if it turns out to be far less interesting than you have been dreaming about. Then you will have to hide your detour from both your partner and from everyone else. It cannot help that people will gossip behind your partner's back – and people will do so if they can get away with it, although they will always claim the opposite! In this case, you should ensure that you are better than even the best detective and erase your tracks as permanently as possible.

Question

What can I do and how should I act if I want to make an indelible impression on a potential future partner?

Is it LOVE?

What would you most like to be loved for – your happy disposition, your winning smile, or your great knowledge of human nature and your phenomenal vision? First you need to be aware of what your own strengths are, and then these must of course be conveyed in the best possible way to the chosen person. But love is not something you can force on another person, for if they do not get it by themselves, you might as well drop it immediately. If the person does fall for you, it must happen naturally, but then you can still try to help things a little on the way by making sure that you can be found in strategic places at the right times so you are not overlooked.

Is it ATTRACTION?

If you only want to have sex with this person, it is just a matter of presenting yourself in the right way so they can get an eyeful of your external merits. But this is just cheap sexual seduction! If you wish instead to get into a long term relationship right from the start, it is recommended that instead you read under the heading

Is it LOVE.

Question

What can I do and how should I react if I feel that we are losing the spark in our relationship?

Is it LOVE?

When people love each other they usually have such a great mutual respect that they can easily talk to each other and express their respective and perhaps divergent views, without the dangers of fighting one another. Therefore discuss how you would like to spend your time together to get some new and different impulses into the relationship. But do not only discuss the practical circumstances when it is actually some horniness that is missing from the relationship. You can read how you can help to regain the attraction in *Is it ATTRACTION?*.

Is it ATTRACTION?

There is often a lack of initiative from both sides to make something other than the usual things happen in the relationship. Maybe it could be you who could find something, and your idea does not exclusively have to relate to sex. It might just be that you need to take a trip into town to see how other people behave. Surprise your partner, get the kids a babysitter and book a table for two in a place where you have never eaten before. You could even go to a belly-dance restaurant or make a sly visit to a little place where you would otherwise never be seen, or go for a spontaneous stay in a cozy hotel at the other end of the country. You should at least try to get away from the domestic pots and pans for a day or two, and maybe as an alternative you need to get away from each other – just for a few days for some variety.

Question

What can I do and how should I react if I am constantly being chased by someone who is very interested in me but who I am not interested in?

Is it LOVE?

You should naturally announce this quite clearly so that the person has no chance of misunderstanding the message that you are not interested in them, and that your personal wishes and needs, as far as relationships are concerned, go in a completely different direction than what this person appears to be able to contribute. Of course it can turn out later that you were horribly wrong about this person, but if they do not have your love and/or personal interest at the moment then that is the most important thing. If you have a partner already, you can always use this as an excuse for your lack of interest – especially if things are going well in your relationship. The alternative is to completely ignore the persistent admirer.

Is it ATTRACTION?

If you do not have a partner who you can stay closer to than you normally would in this situation, you must either ignore the interested person, who has obviously spotted you from a distance, or you must flirt a little with anyone else who might be around. However, make sure in a clever way as early as possible that you announce that the person is *not* appealing in a way that can turn you on, period! Then at least they have a chance to go after someone else during the evening without having wasted all their energy on you.

Where are your Personal Boundaries in the Relationship?

How many people go around waiting for the day to come when everything will work out all by itself and they will have an amazing amount of success – especially in their relationship?

They simply hope that the ideal state will emerge out of the blue and *completely by itself*, but very often these unrealistic people end up having to wait for half an eternity until just a small part of their dreams come true. And so the question is whether it is possible to accelerate this process to some degree, for instance by the people involved taking time to find out what the ideal relationship should be for themselves so that things function in an optimal fashion?

What activities would it feel good to spend time on with your partner, and what is completely inexcusable in a relationship, for example?

Here you are given a lot of questions that can help you to find out where your personal boundaries are in your relationship and in relation to your joint life. However there are no right answers at the back of the book, where you can see whether you answered the questions correctly or not, as

THE CORRECT ANSWERS FOR YOU ARE THOSE THAT YOU REACH YOURSELF !!!

The questions are only asked so that you should think *yourself* so that you arrive unaided at the answers and views that feel right for you regarding relationships, marital and family life – and hopefully your answers will provide quite a clear indication of where your personal boundaries are in everyday life and relationships, and what principles you actually think you should live by in your own life!

In reality no-one on this Earth likes to be dictated to by others about how they should live their lives or what to think about this and that, so here you have the freedom to have exactly what opinion you want. It is therefore recommended that you get yourself pen and paper to write your answers down so that you then can see if there are any places you have contradicted yourself.

Have fun!

Questionnaire

(1)

- How far do you feel it is acceptable that your partner goes in their imagination when they see 'a juicy piece' which makes their mouth water?

- Do you think it is okay to use sexual aids and sex toys in the relationship, and how do you feel about the fact that your partner may get more turned on by what they can do with the equipment than by your actual person?

- Does sex on the fantasy level correspond to physical infidelity, or can these things not be compared at all?

- Do you accept infidelity, and does your answer, depend on whether it is you or your partner who is doing it?

(2)

- If for a time your partner is being boring and not making anything out of either themselves, their own or your shared life, do you have an obligation to put a bit of life back into them?

- Is it your duty to help your partner back to life if they have completely stalled or gone into a bad place?

- Who is responsible for ensuring that both parties

are happy in the relationship and with themselves personally?

- For example, do you have a duty to provide sex in a perhaps moribund relationship in order to put some spark back into it?

- What would you want your partner to do for you if for a time your life were to feel meaningless?

(3)

- Is there a difference between what you are generally attracted to in men/women and what you are attracted to in your partner?

- Is it okay to choose a partner based on how much money and how great a job they have – elements which each in their own way can result in your life together and daily circumstances being more successful, as well as creating the possibility of better realizing your material desires – rather than going after the thing that turns you on the most in a potential partner which you might not be able to control in everyday life?

- Are you looking for safety in the relationship, or do you dare to stick your neck out and bet on the real big love and attraction, which might risk pulling the rug completely out from under you?

- What qualities would you prefer not to choose in the context of a relationship and what would you be less happy for your partner to like in you?

(4)

- Does the outside world and especially your parents' views on cohabitation, security, economics and sex have any influence on your choice of partner and way of life, and if so what?

- Are you very influenced by your upbringing and the way things were done in your childhood home?

- Whose opinion matters most in your life – your own or other people's?

- Was it, is it, or will it be difficult to introduce your new partner into the family and your wider social circle, and would this be in relation to your parents, your children at home, and for your family and friends in general?

(5)

- Is it okay with you that your partner has their own hobbies outside of your joint life together?

- Is it also okay with you if their interest goes in the direction of strip poker, nude bathing, or long vacations to exotic places with friends and *without their partner*?

- Are there limits on how free you should be in relation to each other in the relationship, and if your partner wants to involve you in their personal interests, would you be better off with their choice of interests?

- Is it okay for you to have these interests yourself?

(6)

- Would it be okay with you if your partner lay on the sofa for days on end because there was not any focus on their duties such as chopping wood, minor repairs, mending bicycles and ironing clothes, etc., while you rushed madly around the house trying to meet your share of the duties?

- Is it okay for you that only one of you takes care of the daily chores, while the other takes care of the bigger tasks that crop up along the way?

- How should the division of labor be in the home so that it is satisfactory for both parties and the family as a whole?

- How much should children take part in the chores at home – and as parents/adults do you agree on the current division of labor?

- Are you a good example to your children by doing your stint in the home?

(7)

- Can you accept that your better half visits his or her mother every Sunday to help her with the practical tasks now that your father-in-law is not there anymore, instead of *just now and again* going on a picnic in the woods with your own family at home?

- Perhaps mother-in-law could come with you if she wanted, how would you feel about that?

- Is it okay that you yourself take up a lot of time with your own family?

- Do you feel fine with the prioritizing between 'yours', 'mine' and 'our' family, or do your own parents, your in-laws, ex-partners or various friends and neighbors interfere in your domestic life at home by constantly running in unannounced, so in the end you never have any time for yourselves?

- Have you room for anyone other than yourself in your life, and if so who?

- Can your partner have their own life, or should they only have eyes for you?

- If you have kids, do you give yourselves enough time to be with them?

(8)

- Are you held accountable to your partner every time you buy some new clothes, perfume, darts, billiard cues or a fire truck for the kid, and how is the economic breakdown in the home?

- Is there a difference as to who earns the money and who uses it, and how does this correspond with who primarily takes care of daily chores and shopping, and who has some very inflexible working hours and therefore cannot take part in tasks at home?

- Are you often/always in an economic crisis because of constantly bad deals, or did you just get off to a bad start?

- Can you accept that your partner is stingy in everyday life, while they are happy to pay a lot of money for a bottle of wine when you go out?

- Is it okay for you to save *everything* up in order to take a joint trip around the world or to secure your hopefully joint old age, or do you and your partner generally spend too much money without thinking about yourselves?

- What should the conditions for your joint or individual finances be so that both of you can get by in your daily lives?

(9)

- If you have problems in your relationship or at home concerning children, finances and sex, etc., how do you find it best to tackle the situation?

- Do you set aside time so that you can talk together in the late evening hours when the kids are in bed, and where your partner maybe is sleeping as soundly as the children because he or she have just read a bedtime story – or do you suddenly without warning switch off the TV in the middle of an exciting crime series that your better half is faithfully following every Wednesday to announce that now you should talk together?

- Do you take into account your partner's views

despite the fact that you may deeply disagree with them so that together you can arrive at an acceptable compromise, or do you most want to just beat them up against the wall to get the matter over as quickly as possible and get your opinions across?

- How do you try to resolve the various basic conflicts in the home?

- Is there room for disagreement in the relationship?

(10)

- What good things do you and your partner have to give to each other in your relationship, whether they be emotional, mental, sexual, or material?

- Do you get as much back as you give out and is this important to you?

- Is your relationship functioning satisfactorily according to your measure, or is there a lot/a little that needs to be changed?

- Is the outcome worth fighting for so that the relationship will be better?

- What do you do yourself so that the relationship remains satisfactory and/or gets even better?

- What is the atmosphere in your home like?

- Are you open to each other and do you talk freely about different things, or are there certain topics that are never touched on?

- Do you talk nicely to each other or are you always shouting?

(11)

- Do you have the same sexual needs in terms of style and frequency, and do you respect each other's boundaries in this area so that neither of you go over the line with your partner?

- Have you or your partner ever suggested partner swapping, and did this sound interesting or repulsive to the other's ears?

- Do you and your partner periodically find each other boring, and could this be due to the fact, for example, that when you go to bed you wear the same old worn-out pajamas you have been wearing for the past five or ten years?

- Do you ever make yourself delectable for each other when you go to bed, or when you go to bed are you just looking to sleep?

(12)

- How would you feel if your partner was seriously ill or was out of action in some other way?

- Would you provide them with support in all areas and could you count on a similar gesture from their side?

- Do you support each other emotionally and

mentally if there is a need for this, or have you ever lost sight of this in your relationship?

- Do you talk together, and if so, about what?

- Does your partner listen to you if you are talking about things from your daily life which are of more interest to *you* rather than them?

- Does your partner listen to you in a satisfactory manner, or is it only with half an ear?

- Do you listen properly to your partner when the talk is perhaps technical or philosophical – topics that may not interest you?

(13)

- Do you *always* love your partner or do you just love them on special occasions?

- Are you attracted to your partner?

- What qualities do you find especially attractive and/or repulsive in your partner?

- Do you think you should be/live together for the rest of your life if it was up to you and what does your partner think?

- Have you talked to each other about this?

- Have you secured your future together, and if things go wrong, have you also secured your own futures as well as those of your children?

The Author

Anni Sennov was born in 1962 and is the author of more than 15 books on energy and consciousness, as well as relationships & New Time children, of which several books have been translated from Danish into a number of languages.

Anni Sennov is the woman behind AuraTransformation™ and the Aura Mediator Courses™ (**www.auratransformation.eu**), which since 1996 has become widespread in Scandinavia and in 2007 spread further to the Baltic countries, Finland, England and USA.

Together with her husband Carsten Sennov, she is a partner in Good Adventures Publishing (**www.good-adventures.com**), as well as in the coaching & consulting firm SennovPartners (**www.sennovpartners.eu**), where she advises clients about personal development, energy and consciousness.

Anni & Carsten Sennov have jointly developed the personality type indicator the four element profile™ (**www.fourelementprofile.eu**), which includes four main energies corresponding to the four elements Fire, Water, Earth and Air, which is represented in all people in different balances and strengths.

Anni Sennov originally began her career in the financial world and since 1993 she has had her own practice first with astrological counseling and healing and later with AuraTransformation™ and clairvoyance.

Anni Sennov's work and books are mentioned in numerous magazines and newspapers, and on television and radio in Denmark, Norway, Sweden, Estonia, England, Finland and USA, etc.

You can link to Anni Sennov's profile on Plaxo, LinkedIn, Google+ and Facebook, where she has an English author profile:

facebook.com/pages/Anni-Sennov/141606735859411

You can also subscribe to her English newsletter at **www.anni sennov.eu** and to her Danish newsletter at **www.annisennov.dk**.

Furthermore, you can subscribe to the English four element profile™ newsletter at **www.fourelementprofile.eu**.

Last but not least, you can watch videos about AuraTransform-ation™ at **www.youtube.com/sennovpartners** and on the four element profile™ at **www.youtube.com/fourelementprofile**.

Anni Sennov's Authorship

Current books:

Balance on All Levels with the Crystal and Indigo Energy
Balance på alle planer med krystal- & indigoenergien (Danish)
Balanse på alle plan med krystall- og indigoenergien (Norwegian)
Kristalli- ja indigoenergiat ja kokonaisvaltainen tasapaino (Finnish)

The Crystal Human and the Crystallization Process Part I
The Crystal Human and the Crystallization Process Part II
Krystalmennesket & Krystalliseringsprocessen (Danish)
Kristallmänniskan och Kristalliseringsprocessen (Swedish)

Crystal Children, Indigo Children and Adults of the Future
Krystalbørn, Indigobørn & Fremtidens voksne (Danish)
Kristallbarn, indigobarn och framtidens vuxna (Swedish)
Kristall-lapsed, indigolapsed ja uue ajastu täiskasvanud (Estonian)
Кристальные дети,дети Индигои взрослые нового времени (Russian)

The Little Energy Guide 1 - Co-author: Carsten Sennov
Den lille energiguide 1 - Co-author: Carsten Sennov (Danish)
Den lille energiguiden 1 - Co-author: Carsten Sennov (Norwegian)
Den lilla energiguiden 1 - Co-author: Carsten Sennov (Swedish)
Pieni energiaopas 1 - Co-author: Carsten Sennov (Finnish)
Väike energia teejuht 1 - Co-author: Carsten Sennov (Estonian)
Мини-руководство по работе с энергией, часть 1
- Co-author: Carsten Sennov (Russian)

Andedualitet - Den Nya Tidens förhållande (Swedish)
(Spirit Mates - The New Time Relationship) - Co-author: Carsten Sennov

Karmafri i den nya tiden (Swedish)
(Karma-free in the New Time)

Den Bevidste Leder (Danish)
(The Conscious Leader) – Main author: Carsten Sennov
Bli medveten Ledare i ditt eget liv - Co-author: Carsten Sennov
(Swedish)

Out of print titles in Danish under the author name Anni Sennov:

Planetenergierne bag Jordens befolkning 2005
(The Planet Energies Behind the Earth's Population 2005)

Åndsdualitet - Den Nye Tids Parforhold
(Spirit Mates - The New Time Relationship) - Co-author: Carsten Sennov

Karma-fri i den nye tid *(Karma-free in the New Time)*

Balance på alle planer *(Balance on All Levels)*

Out of print titles in Danish under the author name Anni Kristoffersen:

Åndsdualitet – en bog om kærlighed
(Spirit Mates - A Book About Love) – Co-author: Carsten Sennov

Balance på alle planer *(Balance on All Levels)*

Den nye aura *(The New Aura)*

Planetenergierne bag Jordens befolkning
(The Planet Energies Behind the Earth's Population)

Hvor svært kan det være? *(How Difficult Can It Be?)*

Aura-ændringens ABC *(The ABC of the Aura Transformation)*

Maskulin & Feminin *(Masculine & Feminine Energies)*

Karma-fri og i harmoni *(Karma-free and in Harmony)*

Åndelig energi i dagligdagen *(Daily Spiritual Energy)*

Åndelig Energi *(Spiritual Energy)*

Other books

Balance on All Levels
with the Crystal and Indigo Energy

by Anni Sennov

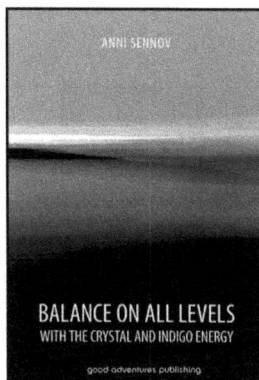

The Little Energy Guide 1

by Anni & Carsten Sennov

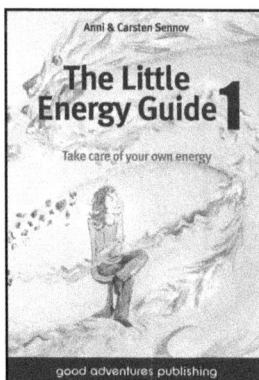

See www.amazon.com / .co.uk and others

The Crystal Human and the Crystallization Process
Part I
by Anni Sennov

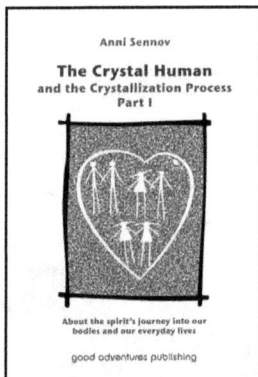

The Crystal Human and the Crystallization Process
Part II
by Anni Sennov

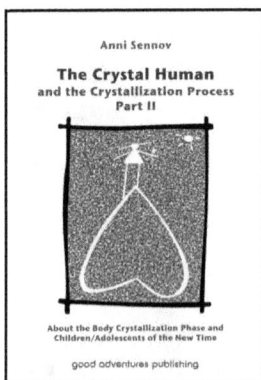

See www.amazon.com / .co.uk and others